T0156686

WALKING
In New Shoes

A Journey of Revealed Truth and Resilience
through the Human Experience

TEA M. HARVEY

iUniverse, Inc.
New York   Bloomington

Walking In New Shoes
A Journey of Revealed Truth and Resilience
through the Human Experience

iUniverse books may be ordered through booksellers or by contacting:

*iUniverse
1663 Liberty Drive
Bloomington, IN 47403
www.iuniverse.com
1-800-Authors (1-800-288-4677)*

*ISBN: 978-1-4502-4148-9 (pbk)
ISBN: 978-1-4502-4149-6 (ebook)*

Printed in the United States of America

iUniverse rev. date: 9/30/10

This project has been forthcoming for some time. I have a fear of success that I work through daily. Through my teachings at Christian Cultural Center, I have learned to manage my weaknesses while I build on my strengths. This work of art is the result of a continuous battle to overcome my fear, not of failure, yet of success. There is so much talent within me waiting for the time of fulfillment so I must press through the thoughts, fears and anxiety with the end in mind. As the end arrive and I feel the completion of the goal coming to a head I get distracted and begin to procrastinate.

There were so many instances in which I got stuck and I would go back and read my writing to help me get out of the ditch. As I began to understand exactly what was holding me back I began to work through the process alone. I told myself that this book had to end. So I had to stop adding poems. Another instance, I decided to share with my editor and friend Swaha Devi after I completed the manuscript. She coached me and helped me get over the hump. Then around the proofing stage I got startled again! The final stage scared me. The publishing company delivered the proof not in three weeks as promised but they delivered the proofs within one week. This meant that I had to perform way before I was ready. I thought to myself, my goal is reaching its fulfillment and then I lost it. My emotions took over. I got distracted and wasted a few weeks. One week before my 35th birthday I spoke to a good friend about it and she gave me a deadline to get it done. I asked for help and Christine Loeffen served as my accountability factor. So I got it done!

With the knowledge of this weakness, I can and will continuously overcome it. Though I do not like when things end, I am aware and accept that all things must come to an end. It is within my ability to speak to myself and change my perspective. So I began to tell myself a story. I sat myself down and said the end is near! The beginning of something new is coming. Those new shoes that you desire to walk in will only be a lamp unto your feet if you allow the end to come to an end. So this is your time! This is your story! Get out of your own way so God can receive the glory. I said to myself, "Climb, crawl and stumble through the doubt, fear and anxiety so God can be a light unto your path." But get it done! *Walking in New Shoes* is a testament to someone recreating themselves for the fulfillment of their dreams. One must keep climbing after each level of triumph, after each height until they reach the point where they can build up the muscle to run in those new shoes. It is an honor to write for you.

Gratitude

I dedicate this work of art to myself. I applaud and celebrate my resilience through this human experience. I am grateful for God's love for He has helped me bring this project to past.

To everyone who contributed to my life along the way I thank you. I give a special thanks to the people who broke me. For my brokenness made a way for my wholeness. Now I am complete not lacking any good thing.

<u>To my family</u>: grandmothers: Carolyn Dyer and Louella Mackey (writer), grandfather: Sloan Dyer, stepfather: the late Curtis Merriweather, brother: Shron Dyer, children: Asurle', Marcus, I'man, Chyna, Marcus Jones and Aleemah Foster, grandson: Amir N. Cato, favorite uncle and friend: Christopher Dyer, mother: Marsha Mackey, father: Gregory Dyer, aunt: Carolyn Dyer, the Booker family, God children: Naquan and Nigeria Gibson and my Marcus Garvey family.

<u>Extended family</u>: Thomas Jefferson Family, Brooklyn Hospital Pediatrics, Dr. S. Chung and staff

<u>To my spiritual leaders</u>: Elder Karen Bernard, Pastor Bernard, Elder Pointer, Christian Cultural Center

<u>To my professors</u>: thank you for the great deposit through history, English, writing at Medgar Evers College, to my professors at Kingsborough Community College......

<u>To my inspiration</u>: Susan L. Taylor, Essence Magazine

<u>To my friends</u>: Keri Watkins (writer), Shaam Jones (author), Karen Elbers (writer), Elona Dotson (author), Marie Eusebe (actress), Lisa Speller, Belinda Boyce, Tynisha Felton, Mickael Johnson, Lisa Gary

<u>Youth at Risk:</u> Christine Loeffen, Kirlyn Joseph, Claudette and Ade Faison, Gary Thompson

<u>To my favorite cousin Mary Booker</u>: I have and still look up to you. You are a woman that I admire and love dearly. You are wise beyond your years and stronger than you can imagine.

<u>To my aunt Barbara Booker</u>: thank you for loving me when I felt like no one else did. You were always nice to me as a little girl and I am fortunate to have you. You are my role model and friend.

<u>To my friend Eshon Payne-Brewer</u>: you are a woman of virtue and value. Warmth, inspiration, sincerity and beauty define you. Thank you for your words of encouragement, motivation and command. For you have spoken things into my life that have helped me get out of foolishness and move to the next level. You add so much value to my life.

<u>To my sister Charnessa Jones</u>: girl I love you! Your laughter, love and commitment to my success have brought joy, trust and thanksgiving to my heart especially when everything fell apart. Thank you for your friendship for it is a gift to me and I am forever grateful.

<u>To my best friend</u>: Kina Battle – on my junior high school diploma case I wrote best friends forever and I did not realize that it would be a reality. Thank you for your unending friendship. Thank you for open and honest communication even when it hurt. Thank you for being a woman of character and resilience. I appreciate that you have not allowed life to harden you yet you shine forth with a warm and open spirit.

Thank you for texting me all night about everything. We are naked and unashamed. We are aware of the ugly parts of our lives, yet still we love each other. How fortunate we are to have one another. Love you.

<u>To my editor and friend</u>: Swaha Devi-thank you for your time, expertise and kindness. Your warm spirit has changed my life.

<u>To my love</u>: Thomas Coleman – thank you for being my friend when everything that ever mattered to me fell apart in my life. You were a bridge when I needed an ear and I am grateful. I love you dearly.

Letters from my heart:

<u>To the reader</u>: As you are reading this I would like to say thank you for picking this work of art up, for opening it up to review its content for taking the time out to come along the journey. It is my desire that you will be empowered, inspired, edified and enlightened. It is my hope that you would pass the baton to someone else in order to empower and inspire them.

<u>To the student</u>: education is more than math, reading, writing and all of the subject areas that you are required to study. Education is life long. It teaches you about life. It helps you to find your place in the world. It fosters structure for your life. It is pivotal in the socialization process thus shaping and forming your lives and worldview. Embrace it, cherish it and make it work for you.

<u>To the teacher</u>: thank you for the miracles that you create daily. Seek to understand and know your students. The bossy ones make great managers/leaders, the talkative ones are speakers, the bored ones are extremely intelligent, those with behavior problems need attention, security and love and those busy ones that can't stay still are so full of life yet they bare greatness within. Partner with their parents to develop what lies within. We love and appreciate your service.

<u>To the parent</u>: when you enter that dark rough place, that place filled with hurt, anger and despair, take your faith with you. In faith you can maintain your peace and peace is pivotal in the parenting process. For with peace you can trust that your children will turn out just fine even if the road gets bumpy, everything falls apart and the

journey is crooked and/or upside down. God has given you your children as your heritage. He hand selected you and equipped you to take care of the children in which he has given you. Recognize the gifts within your children. Pray over them and ask God to help you. Release worry and fear and embrace faith and trust.

To the teenage mother: though I do not promote doing things before its time, you are able to live a life filled with rare and beautiful treasures. I am a living testament to achievement, drive, persistence and structure. It is possible and you are the possibility. It's your life and you are responsible for a life!

To the teenage father: men, we love you and we need you. Seek to understand what manhood is and what it is not. Search yourself and find your way. Be responsible, communicate your feelings, be present and keep trying. Never give up on your child because you ultimately loose yourself.

To the single mother: God has given you everything you need to bear up under the details that go into being a single mother. You are able to train them in the way that they should go. You are a woman of virtue and faith is your anchor. Submit your heritage to God and watch him perform.

To the single father: a man of honor I call you. A king! You are able to take full responsibility for the child(ren) in which has been conceived from your loin. Continue to change history and create a better society by being the model.

The Journey:

While I was *Walking in New Shoes,* I learned that I am *Good Enough. Beloved* is what I am called. So with this knowledge I will *Do the Work* required of me to enhance my *Salvation. Because I Love Him,* I will *Surrender* my will and *Trust* him.

New Birth

Walking in New Shoes   2
Writing Myself   4
A Poem in Progress   6

Identity

Good Enough   10
Façade   12
Where is she?   13
Just be yourself   15
Changing Faces   17
The Measure of a Man   18
There's Only One Me   20
The Misconception of diversity   21
The Present   23

Self Perseverance

Beloved   26
I am Better   27
Affirmation   29
The Courage to Leave   30

Motivation

Do the Work   34
A Loud Silence   35
Just do it   36
Courage   38
Rejection is a blessing   39

You Choose   40
This Moment I Live   41

It's Testimony Time!

Salvation   44
He Found Me   46
Hidden In Grace   47
The Dash   48

Love Concurs All

Because I Love Him   50
Good Morning Smile   52
Love in the Moment   53
Forgiveness   54
It's Complicated   56
Ladies, Assume your Position   57
The Thing about Love   59
Understanding Love   60

Transformation

Surrender   62
Offtrack   63
Be Here   64
Unchained   65
Coming into Womanhood   66
Processed   68
Inner Struggle   69
Up From There   70

Wisdom

Trust   74

Fear   76

Anger   77

Total Peace   78

I need a role model   79

Facing the Day   81

Listen, Your Body is Speaking   82

Universal Sway   83

It is what it is   84

If You Say So   85

Just Imagine   86

All Powerful   87

Eve

His Rib   90

Embrace   92

Will the Women Stand Up?   94

New Birth

All things shall become new

I am
A woman of valor
A woman of poise
A woman of purpose
A beloved woman
I am called

Because I have the audacity to affirm my awesomeness
the audacity to say no without explanation
I have the audaciousness to honor myself in a dishonorable
    world
The courage to stand by faith and not be governed by
    sight or circumstance
The boldness to break down the lies and misconceptions
    prearranged by the oppressor
The guts to liberate myself and then liberate someone else
I am called
Woman, that is
That's what I am

A relentless woman
Unstoppable
Unshakable
I don't run from the wind
I glide alongside until it blows over
I don't hide behind the façade socially masking the
    woman in me
Not my femininity

I embrace my imperfections with grace
Dare not perpetuate self hate
Because I am called

Woman
That's what I am
Though oppression tried to slay me
I am
Though inferiority tried to dismay me
I am
And when gender roles
Stereotypes, prejudices
And discrimination
Pressed and squeezed
Stretched and crushed
I, woman, pick myself up
Shift my shoulders back
Lift up my head
Stand upright
And in weakness and despair
I look life in the eye and I say
I am
Woman
The womb of creation
I shall not be moved
Because to this day forth
I'm walking in new shoes

Writing Myself

Yeah you wrote me off
But I'm writing myself
You called me names
Said I was to blame
A black girl lost
Said my birth was in vain
But I'm writing myself
You try and try
to be the false creator
Trying to write me
Telling my story
consumed by my history
Well I'm writing myself
The old is passed away
Behold, I am new
Dear Jealousy
I'm writing myself
Dear Generational Curse
I'm writing myself
Dear envy
I'm writing myself
Dear all of the negative sons of the enemy
I'm writing myself
And finally, finally
Dear invisibility
Guess what, I exist
In this present moment
I feel invisible no more
Because I'm writing myself
I am the ink
Jesus is the pen
Writing with the end in mind

my inner me
Is standing up tall
To it all
And
Dear Obstacles
Thank you for the opportunities
As I continue to recreate myself
No longer will I write someone else's story
No longer will I write me to fit in society's box
So the next time you decide to write me off
Come bold
But behold
I'm a lady in waiting because no matter what, I'm writing
    myself

A Poem in Progress

I am His poem
Written in His mind
Conceived in His thoughts

I am His poem
God's poem
His written expression
Still being expressed
A poem in progress

To express what he purposed
Complimenting his desires
You see, my daddy is a poet
And I am His poetry

Before the creation of the world
An expression of His story
And of course to His glory

It is in my dance
It is in my hand
It is in my talk

He takes pride in His poem
I write as I am written
I am the written writer
Written to write

He is the hand
I am the ink
Positioned on the path of greatness
Honored by the work of His hands

It is in my mouth to speak healing
It is in my hands to write for him
It is in my feet, to dance with my soul
Intercepting the enemy with my pen
Putting an end to deception

My daddy is a poet
And I am his poetry
His poem in progress

Identity

Know, understand and accept who God says you are....
Make a choice to settle the confusion in your mind
You are made in the image and likeness of God, you are
godlike period.

Good Enough

For Elona Dotson

You are good enough
Say it
Believe it
Breathe it

You were formed and fashioned
Wonderfully
Perfectly
Timely

You are good enough
A work of art sculptured by the hands God
On purpose
With a purpose in mind

Without spot
Or wrinkle
Blemish
Or stain

You are good enough

Though people don't believe it
You are
Though you will never measure up to their idea of you
You are
Though you don't fit into their definition of you
You are
Though society refuses to accept your uniqueness
You are

Just you!
Nothing added or taken away
Be good enough for yourself

Say it until you believe it
think it until you agree with it
live it until your nostrils breathe it

Façade

Façade
laughs the loudest
socially masking the deepest hurt
vibrant in pretense
radiantly impressionable
popularity their frontage

Façade
life of the party
posing
posturing
Parading
the façade

when the curtain falls
when the show is over
when the party is done
when the mask is removed

In the stillness
the laughter is quieted
tears begin frowning

In the quiet place
when no one's watching
terror awaits
anxiety overwhelms
the mind of the one who once laughed the loudest

Where is she?

Scattered pieces
Her essence left unprotected
Vulnerably left subjected
Defeated by external lies
Her truth
It dies
All to her demise

Where is she?

Lost
Searching
Gathering stolen pieces
of herself
Her inner light

Where is she?

She's tired but she's standing
She's been wounded but she's healing
She's in labor awaiting a new birth
sustained by the placenta of grace

Where is she?

At war with hope
Fighting for her legacy
Enduring the pain of hardship
Finding her place again

Where is she?

she is here
still living
still striving
she is working her life out
discovering
renewing

Where is she?
She's embracing her new truth

Just be yourself

Don't pretend
To be a friend
To laugh when nothing is funny
Traveling out of obligation
Just to belong

Just be yourself
Bring your everything
Your fear
Your cheer
Be clear

Know that
You are who you are
You can become who you decide
Ultimately, you can only be you

Not your history
What you used to be
Not who they say you are
Define yourself
for yourself
Or else you give others the privilege

Just be yourself
In a crowded room
When you're all alone
Be real
Not fake
Stand up
Stand tall

Affirm yourself

Be strong
Be weak
Be loud
Be meek

Whatever you need to be
Let yourself be
And just be yourself

Changing Faces

I am whole and complete
Not concerned or moved by what you think
I need to change or rearrange
for your convenience

Criticism and negativity
Gratifying your false image of me
Seeking to destroy and govern me

I am whole and complete
Not concerned or governed by what you think
No longer will I change my face
To complement your bogus embrace

The Measure of a Man

Dedicated to Ronald Smalls

You are a man, an exceptional man

A man beyond measure
Evolving
Made in the image of God
Irreplaceable
You have something special to offer
Prepared with a plan

You are a man, an exceptional man

What you did is not who you are
Your mess is a message within the test
Your best is not measured by your worst
Yet your worst is seed for your best

You are a man, an exceptional man

You are not your mistakes
Though you make mistakes they don't make you
Your mistakes are building blocks
Mere opportunities
Awaiting faith's activation

Run the race
the race marked out for you
Maximize your potential
Not captivation
bound by dissention and persecution
Use your mistakes to serve you
to liberate others

You are a man, an exceptional man

Were counting on you
Give your best
Watch God do the rest
In the midst of distress
Reach out
Reach down
And pass the baton to those looking up
To you
An exceptional man

There's Only One Me

There's only one me
Purposed and positioned on the path of greatness

There's only one me
Greatness that will change the face of humanity

There's only one me

The me that I am
The me that I am becoming
The me that exist beyond my limited thinking

So when I doubt myself
When my self esteem is low
When I feel insecure

I will rest in the comfort of knowing
that ultimately there is only one me

The Misconception of diversity

For my baby girl Chyna

Your multiplicity
Unique ability
Lends variety
To an unaware society
Don't get sucked into a category

This mystery
That blinded eyes fail to see
What you bring
Enhances our culture and evolves our history
Be not consumed by this misconception of diversity
Perpetuated by this falling society

Your
Type
Brand
Kind
Class
What does that really mean?
It really doesn't mean a thing

Being
Dissimilar
Unlike
Another
Uncommon
Something else
Is your gift to the world

Being
Distinct

Unique
and discrete
yeah, I think that's kind of neat!

being different is truly misstated
especially in a world where hate is elevated
diversity is not celebrated
meanings of words are manipulated
false images are created
yet the message is related and clearly stated
that diversity is just not appreciated

so when you start to doubt
the beauty of who you truly are
and the world becomes an overwhelming place
claim your fame and know
that being unusual and special
are one and the same

The Present

You are a gift
A gift to the world given by god
He has given you a gift to share with others
Yet the greatest gift of all is the present
The present moment
In it lie the seeds of creation
It is life unto itself
Today is a day that has never existed
Today is a day that will cease existence after today
The gift of the present is miraculous and you are the
    miracle

Self Perseverance

Self perseverance is not a preferred act nor is it optional!
Self perseverance is a vital component
completing the human experience!

- Tanine M. Harvey

Beloved

Inspired by Dr. Adalaide Sandford

Honor yourself
Beloved
Embrace your wholeness
Bask in your perfectness

Inhale love
Exhale fear
Inhale patience
Exhale pain
Retreat in each breath
Become one with it

Dance with the melody between each heartbeat
As you listen to the quiet whispers
Trust in the presence of grace and uncertainty
Embrace simplicity and your inner beauty
In this moment
Nothing else exists

Make music with your song
Open your air waves
Creating space
for your rhythmic dance
The rhythm created as you dare to honor yourself
Beloved

I am Better

Oh you think you better?
Better than me?
Because you graduated from high school
With honors
then attained a college degree
And don't hang on the street
Anymore

Yes I'm better!
I'm blessed and highly favored
I earned a diploma, college degree
All while parenting my child
I'm going all the way baby
Skies the limit

Far from a thought?
I don't think I'm better
I know!

Not better than you
Better as a person
No longer a bitter person
Controlled by anger
Living a low life
In the gutter
At the bottom of the barrel

I am better than when I was self destructing
I am better now
Propelling light into this dark world
Maximizing my potential
For your bare eyes to witness

The potential you see in me
Is in proportion to the same potential in you

I am better
And getting better daily
Living a right kind of life
of love
Sacrifice and forgiveness too
These are the gifts that I give to you

I no longer consume
I contribute
No longer diminish
I build
Goodness and mercy are a garland around my neck
And sweet love binds them all together
So this day
I say and tell the world
Rejoice because I am better
Not better than you
Better to show you the way
So you can be better too
It's all up to you!
So what you gone do?
Yeah, you?

Affirmation

What matters is the story I tell myself

My actions are my responsibility

I draw things, people and situations that dominate my thinking

I have options in regard to how I handle conflict

Some things are worth my time and others are not

I choose the value I place on things

I can be selective in how I spend my time and who I spend it with

During conflict I will focus on the big picture while listening for wisdom

I will not get distracted by irrelevance

I will consider the thoughts that are creating my world

Even when my attitude is wrong I will exert my power and authority with respect and maturity

Power is mine, not through struggle, but through obedience and humility

Obedience comes before understanding and is based on trust

The Courage to Leave

Dedicated to Tanine

When people say they don't want you
When people show you that they don't value you
When time and time again your needs go unmet
When you are faced with silent hostility and indirect
    abuse
It's time to leave

When the liabilities outweigh the assets
When people take away from your wholeness
When they tell you, you don't have anything to offer
When your contribution fail to meet their unrealistic
    standards
It's time to go

Don't stay for the sake of anything
Nothing and no one is that important
It costs too much
Your mental health deserves a shot
Though you take things into consideration
Use wisdom, knowledge and understanding

Don't stay for the kids
for your own selfishness
Don't stay for the money
for your own security
Don't stay in fear
find the courage to leave

Leave that job, projecting its hostile environment on your
    well being
Expecting you to check your humanness at the door

Leave that toxic relationship
Let it go
When you let it go you say yes to new possibilities
Clearing the passage for something new
For the root of Jesse to sprout up
Attracting something greater than your previous
    experience
Something beyond your imagination

You deserve a lifetime of rare and precious moments
Because you are rare and precious
You are valued, loved, wonderful and complete
Know in your heart of hearts that it's already alright
It's perfectly ok if you are rejected, not accepted
Be well with it
there is much gain in loss
know that it is truly their loss
Maybe it was only for a season
The purpose of the thing may have changed
And know
That it's ok for people to change their mind about you
It's not ok for you to change your mind about yourself
Don't leave before it's time
Yet don't stay well over when the time has passed
It takes courage to leave

Motivation

Be inspired, Be Driven, Be Motivated
Allow love to be your motivation

Do the Work

Everything you need lies within
You are....your dreams
Waiting on you to take it
Your goals
Waiting on you to make it
Your life
Waiting on you to take control of it
You have everything you need for life

Don't stand still
Forward movement
You are the possibility of possibilities
The book and the reader
The student and the teacher
The vision and the visionary
The singer and the song

Your dreams, your goals, your life is waiting on you
Believe it
See yourself in it
Live it
Reach for it
Search for it
Do the work
The work required to fulfill your destiny

A Loud Silence

It's not a big deal
They said
Let it go
Stop whining
It is a big deal if it matters to you!

Listen internally
The stillness speaks with a gentle loudness
Guard the wellspring of your heart
Recognize your sensitivity
Discern the signs
Your feelings are essential….the essence of you
Own them
Examine them
You are worthy

With clear resolve
Eliminate the what, the who or is it you
Causing conflict in your soul

Birth something new
Release it and forgive
Renew your mind, body and spirit
And live
On that is….

Walk in the confidence of your own authority
Be a well of thanksgiving
And a fountain of laughter
Understanding the loud voice of your silence

Just do it

Yesterday's menu served focus within
An appetizer of sadness
The main course of doubt
And a side order of despair
Searching to find a sip of faith
A taste of grace

Then inner self met you
At the coffee shop in the back seat of your heart
She heard your wellspring burst forth
Beckoning to your call
She brought dessert along
A taste of encouragement
The sweet luster of hope
And a pinch of wisdom

Confidence, a sweet aroma, filled the shop
As the fragrance of belief entered in
She spoke with urgency
Saying, focus within

Your ingredients are not mixing well
Your life is not working for you
You've been on speed dial
Doing what the world expected
While your heart pumped on the outside

So today
Reposition yourself
Meditate on your heart's desire
Be renewed

Do it in spite of what people will say
In spite of confrontation and challenges
In spite of failure and loss
And in the midst of fear and stress
Whisk up the sweet fragrance of confidence and belief
Letting their aroma fill the shop

Just do it!
Begin again!
Begin a new thing!
Remix your ingredients
Meet yourself in the front seat of the shop

Then roll out the red carpet
As you serve your life with a sprinkle of grace
a meal of honor and a lifetime of self-love

Courage

For my niece Ashley

Courage is moving forward in the midst of defeat
Accepting what you have while you create what you want
When the odds are against you
Courage will stand
Stand alone if necessary

Courage will take that seed, that idea and cultivate it into
    a tree
One that will outlast; one that will leave a legacy

Courage removes the comfort zone
Moving into the unknown
Embracing change
Removing excuses
Courage grabs hold of fear
Giving breath and wings to your dreams

Courage is willing to fail in order to succeed
Courage speaks life into itself
Encouraging itself

Courage says
as long as the breath of life breaths into my nostrils
I will continue…..
To live by faith and not by circumstance
Continue to move forward in the midst of defeat

Rejection is a blessing

Yes the pain
Leaves a stain
Altering the brain
Leaving you drained
Almost insane
In your frame
Of mind that is
So although the sting of rejection burns my dear
Have no fear
Cast your care
Embrace cheer
And understand that through it all you are still here

You Choose

Talk to your depression
Acknowledge it
Own it
Feel it
Be consumed
But dear
Not by your fears
Not by your years
of failures and mistakes
be consumed with your present
bask in the moment
Yeah you failed
Yeah you mistook
Keep living and you will fail
You will mistake some more
But honey
Life's a paradox
You know, sort of inside out
People who fail
Have succeeded because they tried
People who make mistakes
Grow wise because they learn from them

So, talk your depression down
Beat it at its' own game
Compete for your life
It's trying to wear you out
Wear it out with your resistance
Let it go, you have work to do
and baby, bottom line
you can't allow depression to get the best of you
and at the end of the day
you must choose

This Moment I Live

Time is a fleeting vapor
Whisking by
It waits for no man
Time is but a moment

The stage of life is set
From birth to death
How we live is our test
Whether in happiness or in regret

Our caskets will be filled…
Some with broken hearts
Buried potential
unforgiveness, carrying others with them

We will die with many reasons yet no excuses
Why we failed to accomplish
And who stood in our way
What our parents did or did not do

But there will be some who say…
This moment I live
And in this moment
I will forgive
I will live my life
And become the me that I am destined to be
Not wasting any of it on worry or fear
or consumed with the past years

I will appreciate the moment
Honor the gift of the moment
Cherish the tenderness of the moment
Be here in the moment
And seek the fullness of this moment

Oh the moment
How precious it is

Grasp its profundity
Snatch the opportunity
Meet challenge at the front door
Allow your inner light to lead
Maximize each moment aware that this is the only
    moment

This moment is the moment that I live

It's Testimony Time!

I have a story, I have a history, I have a testimony
And I'm grateful that I'm here to share it

Salvation

It was 1997! He sent a friend who called me and said, "get up let's go to church". I said, "No I have a hangover." He pressed me and finally said, "get up I'm coming to get you." He came and I went and I found my salvation.

He came and found me
He lifted me
Off my bed of drunkenness
Whispering softly
Daddy's here

He came and found me
Reached out his hand to me
Bathe me in His presence
Saving me
Lovingly

When I was lost
He came
In my sin
He came
When my worse was at its' worst
He came and he found me

His grace was sufficient for me
His mercy was available to me
daily
His embrace enveloped me
His blood secured me
As his shadow hid me
His love rescued me from myself

His love
oh his love
just loved on me
Sacrificially, redemptively and unconditionally

He knelt before me
Caressing and washing the residue off of me
He held me
Cradled me

I cried out for him
Wrestling in my sleep
Wishing the terror of life would soon disappear
Became too weak to handle the overwhelming fears
So I washed His feet with my tears

Then he came and he found me
He answered me
Openly
In my darkest hour
His light worked on me

He gave his life for me
That I may live life
Life more abundantly
Eternally
He is my salvation!

He Found Me

I remember that night, I remember that week-I was wrestling in my sleep and crying out to God to save me, help me- I said "I'm tired." I did not understand what that meant yet that night He came it started a new life, leaving old things behind-I traded it all for Him. I stopped drinking, left my apartment and I began praying and living better.

When He finds you
Your song keeps singing
Your joy is unspeakable
You are not moved by
malady or tragedy

When He finds you
The search is over
The void is filled
Your soul opens up
The content of your heart is revealed

When He finds you
You'll know
Because His presence will tell you so
His voice is gentle
He answers with peace
Balance will be established
Disorder will cease

When He finds you
Gratitude and thanksgiving will overflow
Old habits and bad attitudes begin to go
and your life will mold
into the vessel of honor He chose
Behold! The moment He finds you!

Hidden In Grace

During rehearsal for the play "The Poet's Testimonies" I needed to be alone.   I sat in the empty sanctuary and cried a hard cry and this is what came out:

I left you for a man again
Now I'm frustrated because I thought I learned my lesson
My worth
No longer hidden behind the veil
I know my worth in you
It's evident by each nail
The nails you took for me
You on that cross
Now each time I leave you
I feel great remorse
For all the nails I put in you
And yet still you love me through

You say "daughter come back to daddy"
With your gentle and loving voice
I'm right here waiting
But Princess it's your choice

I know your heart
You hear my voice
Let's come back together
Reunite, fellowship and rejoice

You are my beloved daughter no matter who you pursue
And baby no doubt my grace is sufficient for you
But time waits for no man
Grace only lasts a while
Come home to daddy
Trust in me and know you are my beloved child

The Dash

When my life is over
I want to leave a legacy of love
A word in season that changed the course of your life
A helping hand cheerfully giving
And rich in thanksgiving

When my life is over
I want to be the change agent
The womb of greatness
The Eve of compassion

When my life is over
I want to be the angel that stretched you beyond your
        reality
I want to be a vessel that led you to your destiny
A symbol that shaped and formed the pieces of your
        puzzle

When my life is over
I want you to know that everything that ever mattered to
        me was you
My life was given to me for the benefit of you

When my life is over
I want the world to be better because of my short stay
I want the dash between my birth and death to read
Well done good and faithful servant!

Love Concurs All

Love is patient and kind; it is with patience and kindness
that one can overlook our faults and see our needs

Because I Love Him

Because I love him
I will stand
take persistence and loyalty by the hand
Stumble through the pain
Walk through the strain
Because I love him

Because I love him
Patience will be my governor
Joy will be my guide
Understanding will be my rule
Because I love him

Because I love him
I will overlook his faults
Polarize the best in him
Respect the man in him
Understand his individualism
Because I love him

Because I love him
I will cherish him
Honor him
Cater to him
Sacrifice for him
Speak highly of him
Stroke him
And make him feel like the man that he is
especially when he loses his way

Because I love him
I will cloth myself in grace
Season my words with maturity
Be led by the light of kindness
Prance in the shoes of peace
Allow compassion to be a garland around my neck
Drench him with the perfume of tenderness
All because I love him

Because I love him
My love will take him to new heights
Expose his hidden gifts
Inspire his creative impulse
Bring out the giant in him

As iron sharpens iron
I will stretch him
Help him
Be a living vessel with him
Be ever praying for him
Just because I love him

Good Morning Smile

Inspired by Thomas Coleman

I love seeing you in the morning
You make me smile when nothing is funny
Shining laughter through the window of my soul
An inner tickle

When you enter a room
My world is alright
I want to take hold of you
Envelope you in me
Deep down where only I
Know how good it feels

I feel your spirit
It surrounds me
I carry you in mine

When we embrace
We become one
Within the walls of desire

Connecting
spirit, mind and soul

I love seeing you in the morning
It makes me smile when nothing is funny
Good morning smile until we meet again

Love in the Moment

Our love story
ended before it began
Though short lived
Our encounter was pleasant
The chemistry was strong
The connection even stronger

Our love story
ended before it began
I miss the possibility
The possibility of you and I
The you and I that never became we
Mourning the loss
Experiencing the separation
Of what little time we shared

Though I mourn
I smile
With thoughts of our love
Our love in the moment
Because in my heart you're still my King
In my mind I'll always be your Queen

Forgiveness

After all you've done to get hurt in the end
Opened your heart because he was your friend
The pain gets so deep til you can't get any sleep
Can't muster up the energy to get a bite to eat
Wishing that the healing process would begin
Streaming down your cheek, those big burning tears
Reminiscing back on the good ole years
The days are gloomy and the nights are blue
Fear says you'll never make it through
But I know a God that has worked it all out
So declare your victory without a doubt and then shout
Count it all joy, he carried you through
Thank the Holy Spirit who gives wisdom to you
Circumstances arrived as part of his divine and perfect
    plan
Have no fear, my love; you're in Jesus' hands
It takes love and faith to forgive your offender
Give it to God- My sister
surrender
Remember your character will always be challenged
But seek God first not revenge
Call on the Lord to strengthen your inner man
So through trails and temptations you can stand
So take a look at you before you judge
Forgiveness is the key don't hold a grudge
The enemy has destroyed and stolen enough
So open your heart and get back your stuff
God gave us forgiveness as a gift
When you embrace love, your perspective will shift
Acquit that man and set him free
God forgave us although unworthy
Always look for the good and not the bad

Embrace love and faithfulness, but don't be had
I believe that God changes people and
God changes things
Get cleansing of your sins and experience what freedom
    brings
Humble yourself unto the Lord
Let's unite in the body on one accord
Our father desires perfect unity
So get prepared, the coming of God is soon to be
Love is measured by the degree of forgiving
So stop just getting by and start by living
He loved and saved us and now we're blessed
So girl make a message out of your mess
Through his grace we have been saved
Through his blood our sins have been waived
Now set some boundaries and take control of your life
Remain in good character and cease the anger and strife
After all you've done to get hurt in the end
Next time open your heart to a qualified friend

It's Complicated

I could act like it doesn't bother me
Being rejected doesn't hurt, you see
I could get busy doing things
Shifting my thoughts and behaviors
Intentionally avoiding what really doesn't bother me

Or I could be real
About what I truly feel

I could act like it doesn't bother me
Being rejected doesn't hurt, you see
Knowing that deep down inside
it really matters to me
The rejection that really doesn't bother me

Ladies, Assume your Position

I am a lady
I know my rightful position
I am not the seeker
I am sought out

I am a lady
I shall not seek my mate
But be prepared for his arrival
Keeping my house in order
Maintaining righteous standards

No longer will I give up parts of myself
Creating universal drama
Investing my precious time and tears
Looking for love outside of me

If interested he'll call
If not, he won't do a thing at all

So ladies
Sisters
Women

If you are seeking
Seeking a man
Reverse the search

Seek your truth
Your beauty
Your divine gifts

You are a good thing!
And he that finds you is blessed
Blessed with the gift of your understanding

Anticipate his presence
Prepare a place for him
Welcome him with an open heart

Yet know your place
And assume your rightful position
And be sought out
not the seeker

The Thing about Love

Although they lie within I don't have all of the answers
Situations and circumstances arise to show us who we
    really are
We are not complete without the social reciprocation of
    another
You are my mirror, exposing my imperfections
My love is fragmented
Not whole
Far from perfect
I am learning how to love you as the season of our
    relationship changes
As we change in it
I must learn to love the new you
I must learn to throw off the old ways of responding and
    reacting to you
But it takes time

Although they lie within I don't have all of the answers
My love is fragmented
Becoming whole
Be present in the process
Trust
That I love you
That I want you
That I have the best in mind toward you
Make room for improvement
Extend a portion of understanding
Douse me with a bit of grace
As we live out the questions while we anticipate the
    answers

Understanding Love

Love with your head not with your heart
Your heart is flooded with emotions
Love is not based on emotions
Love is the result of a choice

Love with your head not with your heart
We often say let your heart lead you
Open your heart and take your head along the path
Drench yourself with knowledge, wisdom and
      understanding

Love with your head not with your heart
Employ consciousness in thought, word and deed
Be mindful of your limitations, your humanness
Allow God to lead you toward love as you learn of Him
And bask in His perfect love

Transformation

He who bounces back will win the prize
He shall triumph through perseverance and persistence

Surrender

Down and out
At the end of my rope
I've prayed
I've cried

Down and out
At the end of my rope
All prayed out!
All cried out!

And now
I'm letting go
Believing
Trusting
Surrendering
Because where I end
Is where God will begin

Offtrack

Starin at blank pages
Seething through the sadness
Searching to find out why
Why I'm offtrack
And how to get back

Starin at blank pages
These pages
Mark triumph
Failure as success inside out
Finding a way to be ok with what has happened to me

Starin at blank pages
No script
Or blueprint
I'm in transition
All structure is gone
Displaced

Starin at blank pages
Attempting to get settled
Practicing patience in this process
Trying to get the courage to start again
Dismissing the distractions
Knowing that even in transition
All things must come to an end
In order to begin again

Be Here

I don't want to be here
But I am not released to leave

My feelings are feeling
But feelings are not a fact

I don't want to be here
But if this is where I need to be

I'll stay
until this season comes to an end

Unchained

I may get stuck
But I won't stay stuck
I may get stuck
Fall off
But I won't give up
Life was freely given
And it's my turn to learn the lesson
Count it a blessin
Stop all the messin and stressin
And keep on passing the testing

I may get stuck
Don't believe in luck
Giving being perfect up
But striving for a way up
A new level
Perfectly speaking
So though
I may get stuck
This life of twists and turns
Can't keep me
The giant in me free's me
The world can't hold me
My ambition runs too deep
I dare not allow this muck to keep me stuck

Coming into Womanhood

Coming into womanhood
My soul is crying out
Thoughts of generational curses
Lies
Experiences
Tears cascading
An awakening

Coming into womanhood
My soul is crying out
Assessing
Cleansing
Revealing
Opening up

Bringing consciousness
To what's working
What's not
Who can stay
Who cannot

Coming into womanhood
Do I consider another opinion
Or do I follow my instinct
Learning my own truth
What's right for me

For the first time
This time
I am coming into womanhood
Desiring to fly on my own
Designing a life
My life
Discovering my beauty

Coming into womanhood
So many changes
At the brink of critical decisions
Unchartered ground
A delicate moment
But it's necessary that I step out into womanhood

Processed

I was an empty shell
Whole on the outer layer
The façade
Fragmented on the innermost layer

My soul
universally scattered
disconnected

watching the pieces of me return
fostering redemption
filling the shell
completing the puzzle

Inner Struggle

I was trying to break the cycle
And the cycle broke me

I was trying to break the cycle
of dysfunction
And life beat me down

I was trying and trying
To get a breakthrough
Until I reached my bottom

Because the cycle broke me
my brokenness made a way
For me to break the cycle that broke me

Up From There

I may be down
But I won't stay here long
May be discouraged
But courage is on the rise
My faith may waiver
But the root is too deep

My self perception
God's vision concerning me
Keeps me going!
Keeps me trusting!
Keeps me believing!

I may be down
But I won't stay here long
God's ability in me soars
The giant inside refuses to rest
Knowing that he is in the midst
of this test
his best
Interest is my success

Now is the time
to rise up
To step out
Live in the possible

So today
If you are down
Know that the way up is down
Get up and get ready!

Move beyond fear
Live in anticipation
With great expectation
Not in apprehension

Get up from there!
<u>Before you stay there too long!</u>

Wisdom

Wisdom will protect you, balance will preserve you and understanding will mature you

Trust

Trust is a choice
A necessity to any entity
Foundational for building
The art of establishing

Trust
It is a choice
In it lies indescribable power
Without it the possibilities remain ambiguous

Like building a fortress on sinking sand
The root is unstable
It's like a city without boundaries

Trust is a choice
Earned through actions
Yet lost in the gust of raging winds
Misunderstandings
And false perceptions

Guard it with discernment
Speak to it in wisdom
Search for it beneath the residue of your past
Understand its' profundity
Intentionally

Trust is consciousness
Waiting to be
Attained
Maintained
and at times regained

Trust is always a choice
Its multi dimensional
Whether we decide to trust or we decide to be trustworthy
It is still a choice

Fear

Fear
Has an agenda of its own
To keep you captive to the unknown
An illusion symbolizing your awaited dream

It keeps you waiting with great anticipation
For the false impression to materialize
Let go of the lies

Your fear is here
Fostering oppression
Tampering with real evidence

Face it
Understand the root of it
Rid yourself of it
As you make room in your life
For the authentic

Anger

You have the power
Housed in a body
Anger has the spirit
Seeking and needing a body
Anybody

So you unconsciously
Allow that demon anger
To take up residence in your mind
Spreading its incurable cancer through your body
Ceasing to ease your life
Overwhelming you with strife

Controlling your emotions and motivation
Creating misdirected and unnecessary situations

You have the power
But you continuously give it away
To that
blood sucking
Vein poppin
Dream killin
Non-stoppin
Demon Anger

Now you are powerless
Fully dis eased
And the sad thing is
your master anger
Is mastering your family and friends too
Destroying their lives
By working through you

Total Peace

It is your peace that the enemy is after
If he can steal your peace
He can kill your faith
Anything without faith is dead

Though we've been given peace
It's our choice to keep it
Hold on to your peace
Don't give it away

It will guard you
Protect you
It is
Uninterrupted by fear
Unshaken by situations
Unmovable by people
It is an assured peace

This peace that stands still on the inside
Not disturbed by the winds of life
It is the giant in me
That keeps me
While everything crumbles at my feet

My peace is my rock
My anchor
My peace is my all
Give power to your peace
Walk in total peace today
And cast your cares on God

I need a role model

From the heart of a child

Live the life
Don't just preach about it
Teach me integrity
By living it
Through your choices
Stop the chattering
And politicking
Don't just set the bounds for me
Live within them
Discipline me with love
And consistency
Show me you love me
Then you can reach me
Teach me and guide me
Listen to me
Hear what I am saying
What my actions are conveying
Don't abuse me
Gossip about me
Label me
Crazy
Out of control
Be patient with me
Be humble and admit when you err
Love me
Accept me
Be fair with me
To love me is to respect me
validate me don't just tolerate me
Don't hate on me
Reduce me to the level your frustrations

I am counting on you
To show me the way
Train me how to live
Forgive me when I do wrong
Live the life you want me to live
Be the model
I do what you do, not what you say to do
So ease your expectations of me
My heart and mind are developing
Live the life, don't just preach about it

Facing the Day

Arise
Face the morning Sun
Choices to make
Emotions
Hormones
Decisions
the details
The cares of this world
Things to do
People to call
Bills to pay

Facing the day
Pondering the wrong
Basking in the blessings
Arise
Face the morning Son
Internal messages say
Speak to the day
Call forth a pound of good thoughts
A spoonful of optimism
An ounce of joy
Greet the day
Ask for help
Arise and face the morning Son
Choose
Decide
To give back to God what he has freely given to you
The Day
This Day
Arise and face the day
A day called today

Listen, Your Body is Speaking

Listen to me
Your body is speaking
Shouting, screaming, stomping
For you to listen
I need you to listen to me
Heart needs healing
My song stop singing
And my dance is at a stand still
Mind overwhelmed
Pullin me here
Pullin me there
My past is kickin up
The present is present
I'm hungry, neglected and tired
Haven't seen you in weeks
The job
The kids
Relationships
They all need you
seeking your attention
But I need you
And believe it or not
You need me too
Your limbs, your heart, mind and soul
Are longing for balance
Longing to be heard
Exercise me
Feed me healthy thoughts and healthy foods
Indulge me in positive environments
I'm dying without you
Take care of me and you will be well to take care of them
Listen to me your body is speaking

Universal Sway

Life is uncertain
Yet there is wisdom in uncertainty

Release your desire
Deliberately
With bravery

Sway to the tempo of your intention
Ballet with the feet of the universe

As you
Recognize
Understand
Trust
expect
and wait
for the manifestation
In the face of uncertainty

It is what it is

There is a season
There is a time
There are patterns and levels
Shifts and changes
Gains and losses

Everything is orchestrated
Universally so
Playing to the melody of the time

Things happen in their time not in your time
Be at peace in the process
Let patience be your armor

Embrace the gift of contentment
Detach from the outcome
Let it be what it is

Therefore
I speak
To the season
To the time
To the universe
Continue to orchestrate the melody of the time
Because ultimately
It is what it is!

If You Say So

If you say so
It is so

Your power
Yet mysterious
is beyond measure

Your creative power employs and organizes
the universe to answer
Your thoughts
Your desires
Your words
creating the space where you find yourself

Proceed with caution
and know
You possess the power
giving the universe permission

If you say so
It will be
Your thoughts and words create your world
be mindful
positive or negative
since either way
the universe will respond

Just Imagine

Imagine a world
In which culture and diversity is embraced
People stand side by side regardless of race
A place where our elders are respected
No longer left destitute and neglected

Imagine a world
without situational ethics
Life degenerating politics
High statistics
all due to covert selfishness

Imagine a world
Without stereotypes
Gender roles
Injustices
Avoidable crisis

Imagine if
Love is our ruler
Peace is our governor
Patience is our guide
And Understanding is our policy

Just imagine what this world would be

We already live in this world
This world resides on the inside
On the inside of you
On the inside of me

All Powerful

Speak to your thoughts
Tell them what you want them to say
They are ever speaking
Throughout the day

Speak to your thoughts
Direct them in the way they should go
You have the power to tell them no
And the ability to let them go

Speak to your thoughts
Thoughts derived from fears
Thoughts of memories that hinder you from past years

For the battle begins in the mind
Tell them to flee
Be renewed in time
Plant a new and fruitful seed
That will come to pass indeed

Speak to your thoughts
First a thought, then a word, then a deed
Before you know that thought is no longer a seed

All power belongs to you
Think about what you are thinking
As you consciously
Think yourself into your desires

Eve

WILL THE WOMEN STAND UP!

I call you out of darkness woman!
Young women, old women, rich women, poor women,
single women, married women, slim women, thick
women, black women, white women, immigrant
women, homeless women, molested women,
abandoned women, widowed women, fatherless
women, barren women, sick women, lost women,
business women, Christian women

♀

I Call to You
I call on your belovedness
I call on your wholeness
I call on your perfectness

His Rib

Inspired by Arnold Pinder

For no suitable helper was found
For she was made from his rib
What God took out of Adam
He never replaced
For it is good for man to have woman
His own woman
Custom fit for him

And what better place to create a woman suitable for him
Than from his own loin
And after he created her he brought her to the man

And the first words he spoke
Were words of acceptance
Words of identity
Words of love
She shall be bones of my bones
flesh of my flesh
Then he named her woman
Because she was taken out of himself
For this reason man will leave his family
unite with his wife
Forsaking all others
and the two shall become one

His rib
His completion
His assistant
She is his woman
The womb of all creation

With her understanding
He is blessed
With her wisdom
He is blessed
With her respect
He is blessed

For she is his Queen
The heart of their home
As he is her King
The priest on the throne

Her protection
Her provider
The man who walks beside her

He loves
Directs
Disciplines
Protects

Together they are royalty
Together they are man and woman
Together they live in unity
creating a greater harmony

Embrace

Am I my sisters' keeper?
Y.E.S.!
The sister I know
The sister I do not know
The sister I do not like
Nor understand
Yet I am her keeper
The one I hold in my hand

Am I my sisters' keeper?
Yes I am
Dare not step in the way
of what her hands built
and her heart holds

Whether we've met or not
You are my sister
and I feel your heart
I have your best in mind
and I'm committed to my part

Am I my sisters' keeper?
Yes I am
How could I dislike you?
When we are the same
How could I discount you?
When we bare the same name

How dare I allow bitterness
To govern our sisterness
Though we may not always agree
Sisters are eternal
Let's take this one for the team!

Woman is what we're called
And that's who we are
Now, once and for all
<u>Let's allow *LOVE* to cover each and every scar</u>!

So sister, my sister
Come forth and take my hand
Let's unite and walk the path of God's perfect plan

Will the Women Stand Up?

Dedicated to all the beloved women

I am a Woman first
How dare I step into your life
Cause you unjust pain and strife
Cut your heart like with a knife
When I already know you are *HIS wife*

He's not mine
So no need for me to act blind
Though temptation may come for a time
I am all Woman!
And that's the Bottom line!

Even if your man is a dime
Stealing from another woman's household
Last I checked
Is still a crime!

It goes against the grain
Even though his offer came
The woman in me shall never claim

He can only cheat
Upon my consent
His offer will not stand
Cause sister, I'm committed to God's perfect plan

Your family I shall not shame
And in the end of it all
I am to blame

Yet I know my position
I have no right to your investment
I am a woman first
A woman before anything!

The Authentic
Dedicated to our children

It is the mother in me that cannot see
You being anything to me
When you fail to claim your seed
Your child
Your heritage
That which come from your loin

How do I commit to you?
When you deny the essential part of you
Those little faces that depend on you

How do I lay with you?
Share time and experiences with you
Spend money with you
Taking away precious moments
That could be shared with the two of you

You and your child
The child that bare your name
How dare I claim!
To love a man with great disdain
causing her mother unjust pain

How do I
Woman
A MOTHER
consent to your lack of fatherhood
When I the same woman
fall victim to the same bull

I am a mother first!
The authentic!

It's been revealed
My position toward you
Please get out of my face
Your vile act is crowding my space

So go your way
Steady on the prow
Yet make a mental note, brother
That my commitment is to your child!

Notes

_____
_____
_____
_____
_____
_____
_____
_____
_____
_____
_____
_____
_____
_____
_____
_____
_____
_____
_____
_____
_____